TALKING TO SELF

T0078296

TALKING TO SELF

THE TRUTHS OF LIFE

DR. DILLIP KUMAR DASH

PARTRIDGE

A Penguin Random House Company

Copyright © 2013 by Dr. Dillip Kumar Dash.

ISBN: Hardcover   978-1-4828-0157-6
             Softcover   978-1-4828-0156-9
             Ebook   978-1-4828-0155-2

Dr Dillip Kumar Dash
Senior Consultant
Deptt. Of Psychiatry
Apollo Hospitals, Bilaspur
C. G. 495006
Mobile: 91-98271-57323
Email: dillip.dash47@gmail.com
        www.dilipkumardash.com

To order additional copies of this book, contact
Partridge India
000 800 10062 62
www.partridgepublishing.com/india
orders.india@partridgepublishing.com

CONTENTS

DEDICATION

This small book is dedicated to my two grandmothers
who made me realise the splendour of love and life.

EPIGRAPH

Flowers and bees from a different geography silently speaking to a musician we are from the same planet.

—Dillip Kumar Dash

FOREWORD

Dillip has been amiable to all. Behind his bearded persona lies a very thoughtful but extremely jovial nature. But one thing I have always realized over more than a decade or so, ever since I came to know him closely, that he possesses a unique ability to delve into everyday issues in a highly philosophical way. There is a certain universality about his thoughts and writings. He is constantly in search of the divine, the unseen & the unexplained. I wish him all the success. May God bless him & his family.

Dr. Devendra Singh
Deptt. Of Gastroenterology
Apollo Hospitals, Bilaspur

PREFACE

There is so much going on in my mind that I can never pen it all down, as words are not enough to express all my feelings. It is because I do not have a word for truth; it is residing somewhere in my mind. I know people have never tried to reveal the treasure of my love for them. My departure will make them understand the worth of my desires. My desires contain many lives than my words and shall try to make a desert flower, cheer the hearts of people and make their minds dance so that they can live in the custody of the Almighty. This book is a short composition of some of my emotions where I have tried to heal up my own cry and the cry of the entire mankind. However, these are my expressed emotions. I experienced solace, silence at the core of my life, and I tried to put a string from my soul to the heaven where peace remains with all the angels. This book is a pure and honest narration of how I regard eternity, life, and human relationships. All this has been made possible because of my mother's affection, which is the source of my emotions.

Saints like Kabir, poets like Rabindranath Tagore and many others have narrated life in their own words, but the goal is the same—to attain the value of nothingness. This complete depiction is the epic of my entire thoughts and emotions and is not in contradiction to others' views. With all regards I fold my hands before all the great people who have shown me the path of access to the cosmic metaphysical plane.

You have given me a chance to talk and I bow my head before you. However my lips can only spell a few words and those may be only related to politics. People only indulge in politics of honesty and sanity throughout their life. And I believe I do a better transaction of making a garland of a few letters and words. Those are my heart beats, and surely my heart speaks better than my mind. Perhaps till the end of my life, I shall do my job more thoughtfully.

People, throughout their entire life, relentlessly carry disgust, paranoia, and, at the end, they land up in an ocean of depression. This simple book can guide those people who over the years have been suffering and can generate a heart-to-heart relationship with the entire existence.

Every life is full with emotions and experiences which people did not realise. Life is a combination of countless events. Most of us experience life full with miseries, which is nothing but our past experiences.

We play our part without knowing the essence of the act. We rationalise one thing for the other, which is tougher.

It has been my honest endeavour to make people realise that life is incorporated with emotional and spiritual dynamics, beyond which there is nothing.

Through your journey, many sweet memories and spiritual events will come your way, which you must not miss. At the end of the day, you will find the Almighty walking with you.

Dillip Kumar Dash

ACKNOWLEDGEMENT

I am deeply indebted to all my patients because of whose unending inspiration and respect I got an opportunity to write this book. In spite of their debilitating mental ailments, they wait for my consultation till I finish writing a few words. I am highly obliged to them.

I bow my head before the timeless discourses of Osho who certainly is an unseen mentor for me.

I express my honest and humble regards to the CEO, DMS, and all my colleagues and other staffs for their everlasting support to me for writing this book and those earlier published.

I express sincere thanks to the computer assistant Mr Shiv for his typing work.

Love to Ananya Sanjana and Shikshit.

Dillip Kumar Dash

THE ALMIGHTY

Thou almighty! My hands are full with your blessings. This makes me unable to embrace you. Please spread the love you have given me to the next. You come in my heart and soul in the darkness of night and in the dazzling sun at mid-day. Take my earnings and give it to those who are next to me. Let me be deprived of what remains as a barrier between you and me, after which I can embrace you in glee. I can then breathe in solace, and there will be only the huge existence—neither me nor you. It is because of your love and innocence that you bless all of us.

People see you a million times in their life as a stranger, but I have seen you once in this war field and you are repeatedly seen in my thoughts. I have seen you in so many occasions day and night, in festivals, in fairy tales. You blossom in every season and weather, but your colour never fades. Now I blossomed and hope your colour will take part in me forever. This is all about you and your musk.

Silence speaks the highest truths and flows in the blood of the mass. You 'the silence' thrive in all odds. We could never unveil your beautiful face, your glittering eyes. We forget your greatness and live nonsense. The walls of the prison, the trees of the forest also speak about your highness. Alas! We could have heard your silent words and those of 'The Almighty'.

I danced a while; it was your love.

I sang a song; it was your voice.

You danced and sang too; after a little while we were in one platform. Neither you were evident nor me. The song was there, the music was there, and the voice was there, but neither you nor I were there.

Something is there unseen, unknown. Somebody is there a little ahead of the voice of today. A little different may the other day be. We all are same but of different nations—the heaven and the earth. There is no LOC, and like a huge foyer, we all are the same. We ask questions in forums and forget. We stand in the dark and disgust. And we never ask who is there unseen, the unknown.

Once a prisoner said to the king, 'Oh King, you are unfortunate to relish the happiness of the kingdom as you are always surrounded by your pride, but I have become a king as I was protected from a million swords because of the high walls of the prison. My mind was free as I did not have my old sword with me. My freedom was always with the Almighty. My life threats were taken care of by you being the dictator, and I have plenty of time to talk to the Almighty.'

You can also talk to the Almighty when you will be in this small prison rather than in the palace.

A day will come when I shall fetch you and try to hold you in my empty hands, to see you through the high sky and the deep ocean. A day will come when I shall feel your highness and try to dissolve the anguish people have, to see lives not of coercion. A day will come when I shall see their cry turning into a carol. I shall destroy the world of cruelty, dishonesty, and of massacre.

A day will come when I shall fetch you and try to make this world a little more peaceful.

An unsung music comes with the breeze with all your majestic holiness. It strikes in my mind, and there remains only an empty space for peace. Nothing else is felt apart from my heartbeats in which you play your music.

It is the love for you 'the dearest eternity' which shows the path towards your holiness.

The universe is little or limitless. It is unknowable, so is our mind. The energy which I have, we all have and that makes the universe bright. This energy which is within me makes the universe bright and worthy of what it is. So the universe starts from me and each particle of this earth. We all make this universe what it is.

People have made this world a cell of inhuman attributes. I searched in all corners, breaking the walls of the cell to find a place where flocks of birds make their nest. In a festival time I was once walking through the streets near a temple, and I heard the voice of the deity giving blessings to me. In my mind I said, 'God, you have made me conscious. Now I can find a place near a bird's nest.'

All of us have a strong friendship as we are born of the same air and aim. We live day and night with the same breath and beats either in persecution or pleasure. There is togetherness and hostility of facts and fossils. There is tenderness of love in disparity. We dance in ecstasy of unconscious loneliness. But there remains a heaven and an earth. In between, 'you' stay, if not anything.

I pray to God to not just defeat the devils but to make them my neighbours of childhood and a part of the childhood play.

I pray to God to not just to alleviate my agonies but to make my heart and mind strong to conquer the aspersions of my fate.

I pray to God to not just give me success and wisdom but to help me face failures in order for me to become successful. God! You never forget to show me a little light in my failure.

No act is mine; no thought is mine, and no name is mine, neither is any personification.

All are your little plays. I just play like a child in the pursuance of my identity in fear. Sometimes I call my mother and then my mother and I see something which is close to every bit of you the Almighty.

I am sitting here near the door of my cottage till the evening star is seen, waiting for your entry into my small cottage. The birds have taken their way to their nests through the fading sunlight. The flowers have closed their petals, and you have not yet taken entrance to my cottage. It does not matter when you will come as I have already smelt your coming from the fading sunlight. All these have made your presence before you came. It is not my pain of waiting for you to welcome but of the pleasure of my wish to meet you.

The universe composes its music which all planets play. It rings in the ears of flying birds across the sea. They come for happiness in a mass camp and play their music too. Upon hearing the music, the passers-by and the clouds dance in the bosom of the earth. And thou the greatest musician play every day. Amongst all your beloved, some cry for money, while some die for miracles looking at the heavens for your grace.

Many talk about religiosity, so do I. One day I went to a master's hermitage, and he said, 'When all your thoughts of longing for the exterior would vanish, you shall find some empty space in the mind, and that is religiosity.' But religion neither has a meaning nor an existence.

When I shall wake up from the little disbelief, my soul and body will dance in reciprocation. My life shall be for finding the hidden love, and the rest of my efforts would be just for my survival.

The Almighty in a miniature is little different in its existence, form, and flow than in an expanded object or a higher species. However, the evolutionary process always reduces the in-between over all difference. Either we are one step low or up, no matter we shall be reaching there. We are having the same godliness. Kabir, the saint poet, says, 'The mercy of the master will take you to the mighty. For this you have to be full with love and obligation. When the mighty will rain, "the lotus of your heart will open", and then there would be a positive progress.'

It is he who is not sitting in the heaven nor sleeping in the ocean. It is the ambience of the serenity all over, which we do not perceive. It flows all over and forever and does not lose the path or the power. All fall into it some day and merge with it.

It is like a deep ocean and as if it is the first entity in the universe.

It is the ever-flowing power which softens the anguish of people. It dissolves the ignorance.

It is the constructive as well the destructive flow in all living and non-living things. It is both in the positive and the negative poles of a magnet.

It does not do sin nor piety. It is inside of us and outside and is like a black hole. It cannot be understood because it was there before your God.

MOTHER

My village house, paddy fields, coconut trees, and the heavenly blue sky all merge into my mother's love. There were hard days in my childhood. Before dawn, she would clean the utensils left dirty from the previous night and then prepare food. She would hand over my school bag to me near the small temple in front of my house, and I would capture all her sanity and saintly attitudes in my eyes and take them to the school.

I would come with some burden from the school with a lot of homework to do, but my mother would dispel all my conflicts and worries by cleaning my feet and giving me some cold rice and curry to eat. In the evening, she would do *aarti* around a Tulsi plant and then lights the lantern and put a gunny bag on the floor over which I would sit and study. And this is the story of my mother and her pious love for me.

My mother, your sanity and saintly love has made me so strong, which makes me overcome the boisterous tides of life. You have generated faith in the Almighty in my soft heart. Now as I stay alone in my late forties with heavily laden work pressure, you call me telephonically in the night. You still bother if I have had my food on time or not, even though you suffer from your own agonies of physical ailments.

Some day we shall depart from each other. We shall depart from the earth. But we shall meet again in a different world where I shall fall into your lap to take a sedative sleep.

23

I remember how you taught me to walk and to talk; you have taken care of my aloofness in my dreams. Now life has taken its share and our bond is made weaker by the brokers of life. My mother, you took me into your chest, put a cloth around me, and the flow of the flood took over. We are lost in the rising water. Some people bid us a goodbye and some cried. Let me tell the world, I have kept my emotions for my mother. And if those are little less for the world, I shall come again. We all shall join our hands together to save our mother.

You suffer but feed me, leaving your agonies behind, and pour love like the Himalayas. And you do not keep consciousness of your sovereignty. The pain you bear of loneliness at your old age with diseases and disparity—you deny those. And more than these, your hands, with their showering fragrance, remain at the top of my head giving me a shelter in a valley of virtues. As you told me in the childhood fairy tales that our ancestors have become stars in the sky, you would definitely be looking at me from the heaven even after I leave this planet. You shall be even closer to me than each drop of blood in my arteries when I shall see you through my windows on a dark evening.

I asked myself while passing by a graveyard as to why the place was so silent, calm, and even the breeze soundless, but I did not get any answer. And years after when my mother was at the door of almighty death, she told me the graveyard is too heavenly and that she has found a place over there with her dear dead. I searched throughout my life with love for the same place where my mother took shelter, and I found it.

I asked, 'Are they fearful who search love for a living?' And my mother replied, 'Oh yes! They are even more fearful in anticipation of getting love into their life.'

Mother, you create different universes at your own cost. My childhood days are now my treasures of mystical thoughts. I memorise all those through dawn and dusk. Now all those merged and brought a huge smile to my face; it created a few rainbows in the sky and are seen through my windows. *You are seen everywhere.* Even in my difficult days, you were peeping through my windows, giving million hopes of life. You cared for everything. Sometimes I felt sorry for making you unhappy. But the next moment you changed things by spreading rose petals around me. My mother is my entire existence.

Mother, you spread your fragrance from the sky, which touches my heart, giving solace in silence. I stand tall, raising my head as high as the Himalayas, *but it is still under the shadow of your hands during mid-day. Mother*, you care for me so much. When I look into the sky, you are there in blue particles and in each bit of the clouds. I look into the green grass beneath the Tibetan mountain range; you are there in the wavy movements of the grass. You are there in the stones and patchy water around the valley. You feed and serve me, Mother. The cranes silently sit near a lake where everything spreads into you, and there is nothing beyond it. *Mother*, I see you there at the Tibetan huts from where comes resonance of the Buddhist temple *and also from there where no sound exists.*

28

I spread my gaze till you are seen in the horizon. You are left without a piece of cloth. I cry for you, my mother. You have faced serious devastation from all around. Hope my songs and cry will catch you in the horizon. *I have seen your broad arms extended to me from far across the road where nobody remains.*

I have seen your broad arms giving security and sanity to me. The fairy tales you told in my childhood have encapsulated my mind as a kingdom of thrill and impending spring. I fondly remembered those in my adolescent days, still spreading a little smile of joy and making me feel alive. *My mother,* you are living in my blood. *I have seen your broad arms* giving some token money for my college expenses. I saw you graceful even when I left you alone. Now I see my mother shivering with poverty.

Life is a mysterious journey of two breaths. It is already there before you wished to get the same. Wake up and perform the best you can. *Plenty of lives will come your way.* And it will go beyond your wish till nothingness prevails. I wished to feel this nothingness, and it happened when I woke up in the morning from my mother's lap.

I can tell a bit about love. *But my mother can tell you better as she generated love for me.* All of it came from her heart and every drop of blood. I can tell a bit about love, something which I learnt from my peers and parties. These are just words. *But my mother can tell about love better than all.* She took the pain of immortal death for her successor. And her motherhood is deathless.

The flowers with their fragrance, the mountains with their height touch the clouds and pierce the heavens. And it is you my mother who made me learn and understand the beauty of the entire existence. *I have placed the love which my mother gave me in my childhood in my eyes and see love all around. The truthfulness which my father taught me in my adolescent days is in my bloodstream.* But now everywhere, there is only paranoia of bloodshed. My teachers and fellow members who talked about the pride of our soul have all evaporated.

My mother told me that I was too simple and weak to starkly deal with this mystical world. I remember my mother told me that the hurting words were apparent but I would remain under the sheath of my beliefs and the testimony would come a little later and that I would come out of the burial ground even though I was too weak. My mother told me, 'You are weak but can find a way for everything.'

We never possess you; we are in your heart and what is circulating in our blood is your permutation. You desire not any but you hide your sovereignty. It is your mighty tenderness of not imposing your sovereignty on to us.

You cry wilfully.

You perish smiling and believe in us for taking you to a mosque after your death, if not anything else. *You are my mother.*

Beyond all her poverty she remains happy and talks about stories of angels to her children. We in haste talk about love, of not losing our loved ones. And she, in all knowing of your betrayal, sprinkles the mist of love particles to your endless grievances. It is the infidelity which makes marriages constrained, but still we are her offspring although she suffered many divorces; we are rich in her poverty. 'Man is a slave of his own poverty.'

I sometimes got beaten by my mother and there flourished motherhood. I may not have grumbled at her in my ruminations for her beating. And the relationship persisted with her motherhood because of the deathless conception in her womb.

The conversations between you and me are only our past, but our present does not recognise us. We all have forgotten our present relationships with her, and one day we may get to know that she passed away. We shall then miss an opportunity to see her face.

I suffer the bereavement of your departure. But is it more than the soul you provided me? You have provided me a soul beyond all bereavements, and you have quenched my thirst with the milk of your breast, *my mother.* A beautiful life lies in the silent breeze, in the calm ocean, and in the sweetness of your voice.

If I would have been a mother and borne the pain of childbirth, I would have known more of you, Mother. And now you are crippled and thoughtless, blind of the future for which you are shelter-less, hungry, and diseased. But you are still flowering although the seasons have started withering.

You taught me that all things in life happen for a cause or a crime. And everything does have a harvesting season.

I have not forgotten your anguish for me, in my not being obedient. And your punishments made me courageous. I know you are my mother. You love all your children with the same emotions, as all are of the same blood and breath.

THE MASTER

The master said, I am coming to make you awakened;

I shall sing and break your dreams, would not let you hide anywhere;

I am coming here to make your morning fresh, throwing flowers at the rising sun.

Till now you are deluded by your imaginations; I shall break those in your heaven.

I am coming here to show your face in the mirror which is encapsulated by stress; I am coming to give you a fruit of your own. Never be restless, I shall take you to the sands of the ocean.

Break the chain of your illusions; I shall never let you go as a drop. I shall make you an ocean. You wake up, the earth will follow your path and the sky will bless you with nectar. Now I am coming to make you awakened.

The master said to me during my early morning walk, 'Your fear of death is no different than your desire for life. Unless you look into the ups and downs of life, you will also be blind to death. How can the night blinds be delighted of the glow-worms? And hence you look into the fire (energy) of your life and will fall into the valley of death in the hopes of the rain.'

For what do you serve the nation, and for what do you search for miracles? He replied, 'It is only to go into the eternity.'

The next evening during the dinner, the master told that all is for a peaceful sleep; in dreams you can search the truth of your fear.

For what you fear the most is your empathy for others' diseases and death.

And the next morning when people shall bury you, you may sing the song of life again.

Let my heartbeats remain in your hand, and let my thoughts speak of their own. You can carry me a little further, and I can speak to you a little more. When I shall stop talking to you, it would be the time to say goodbye. Let you then stop carrying my heartbeats. I shall come to you with nothing, like a bud into blossoming. And that would be a little like *you the holy master.*

The master said, 'You have awakened from the darkness of the fear. It is now the final touch you give to your words. Now the time has come for a beautiful departure. I would see you in the far distant sky as an emerging star some day. I shall keep all the love in my heart, and you will drop glorious rain all over the world.'

Two friends met each other at the gate of a master's hermitage in a deep forest. And on the path there were fountains and small cold water rivers on the hills, stony roads, thorny plants, wild animals, birds with songs of the jungle, breeze of the baby leaves, and the security of the silent sky. One was fearful alone in the path of not reaching the hermitage because of the threat of carnivores. The other was amused by the beauty of the existence. The master told that one had already gone beyond his hermitage and other to start the journey again.

The master tells regarding Yoga again, as to how it can give a peaceful death and a new life. He says, 'Unless you die, the new cannot be born. Your death will become your new life. Yoga is your total being. It works through your thinking (from head) to your obligation of surrender (from heart).'

To have an actual death, the Yoga principle has to be understood. The first Yoga principle is: 'Now' is the discipline of Yoga.

'Now' implicates the 'mind'.

'Discipline' implicates 'creativity with judgement'.

47

The second principle: No mind state

Mind comprises of all your struggling forces, either positive or negative. In the entire process of mind you are unstable, and Yoga means to become stable and then leads to the cessation of mind. Then only your death will be a second death.

Mind is just a function, and you can make it 'no mind'.

THE SON OF THE LORD

The son of the Lord asked the master, 'Does silence mean remaining mute?' The master replied, 'What you think about silence is remaining mute. It is not my answer. Silence for me is the event which cannot break my peace. My silence is my peace, which is huge. I am in silence always even during my speech, my singing and dancing because these take me more towards the periphery of my awareness of the cult. Not speaking is not silence. It is against words and your mind is always resounding with words. My silence is not the poverty of words. My silence is my presence, and my silence can talk to others. "You the son of the Lord".'

The son of the Lord: You come neither from the heaven nor from hell. You do not possess the sky nor you require the entire earth. There are many planets, beyond which are fountains and fire. They are not to be possessed by the son of the Lord.

The son of the Lord: The prince, a young man of whom the soul unveiled. Soul: The Lord of his own.

The poor, the rich, the dead, and the diseased neither to live nor to die. The son of the Lord: You are thirsty for not drinking, to shower the nectar.

Lord, you have blessed me of not talking too much. Keep me away from all cravings and let my mind be free from all juggles.

The son of the Lord: Here there is a monastery, but there remains no monk. There is a tavern where all are delirious but no one drunk. Hope, the son of the Lord will one day drink the divine. And there will remain a monk, the son of the Lord.

'Life is of millions of events, a chain of merciful miracles. I don't want to close my eyes for a second and miss the life,' announced the son of the Lord.

The son of the Lord: Neither have a friend nor a foe. All of them are living, eating, and miserly passing by the golden gate. It is only the son of the Lord who is hungry, hunted, and weeping on the wedding. It is the day; the Lord is welcoming the son to be divine. It is the son of the Lord, not knowing who is a friend, who a foe.

The son of the Lord: Not tied up by the rope of the illusion, the illusion either of a woman, wealth, wisdom, or witchcraft. You manifest in him who is neither here nor there. You would be in many more planets and in a hut, you the son of the Lord.

The son of the Lord: You need no oil and wick to ignite the lamp, neither to run relentlessly. You have already won the game. The wisdom is there for many more heavens to be built.

It is just a short presence over here. It is not the call of earth; it is the call of my heart to say nothing to you but just smile a serene smile. It's not mine but of the heaven. It's to say to you that you all have loved me and I never knew. It's my miserly presence to meet you somewhere sometime again, the son of the Lord.

The son of the Lord: We can run together a yard or two with love. The heavenly garden and young flowers are all in control of time. There are many streets ahead to run alone. We shall meet a life after, and it's needless to speak about love. We learn in peace to fall down in the control of time.

The son of the Lord: I don't have any reason to count the age. It is he who as a friend with all honesty kept a record. I neither count the dynasty nor the downfall of my ancestors. There were sorrows of loneliness, agony of struggle, miseries of selfishness. But I know you are there to cherish my happiness, to give me company.

Years have passed having not met you. Your departure and life passed like a breath. The knock of death is no less than death. The celebration of my sorrows is no less than ecstasy, and those will make you worried. You come here again to my graveyard; we will rejoice my death and your wish, the son of the Lord.

Let me talk to myself; let me walk alone; let me see through my own eyes. I can see the world better . . . Let me write a few words. I can make a few compositions . . . I know you are there to give the best music for these. I can sing silently in your voice. Let me hear the auspicious sound of your Veena, and may that be the last wish of the son of the Lord.

You have stored so much pain and agony in your mind in the careless moments of celebration of nonsense. Your promise of love for all is eternal for not breaking the tie of endless expectations in the tavern. You know all this, the Lord; you know all those things which are unknown to the son of the Lord.

WALKING ALONG WITH LIFE

I dreamt of life and found myself at the golden gate of an emperor. I thought of life subconsciously and wrote a little about my emotions and there was no king, no empire when I walked along with life. When I thought consciously life was only the eternal silence. The next morning when the poet woke up with a piece of paper to write about dear daffodils, he found the king decapitated.

I spoke to myself when I was alone and aloof with some joy and grief. I believed (of knowledge) the time is the rotation of the wings of the clock. I saw people going to their jobs, doing merciless acts, and offering prayers with piety. And all those are because of waste possessions. I went deep into my sorrows with lonely attributes and found those are my real joys. I found all through my journey of life I was alone but carrying a pious splendour inside.

If you cannot clean a few ugly utensils of those refugees, take my hands and steal those, but let them play their folk in this mystical eve. I have seen the silence of the ocean beyond scale. Let this silence talk to the storms coming ahead not to destroy the camps of these refugees. Many angels come in dreams from the songs with a choir from the heaven. Let them dance a little more with those refugees before they go to sleep without dinner. Let them sow and grow paddy and harvest during the season. We will have a chance to dance and sing to the folks of those refugees. All they do for a happy evening and all you do for a good morning. Let them grow with us; we can give many more angels to the heaven.

In talking to self, I realised all I do is certainly not destructive. In every act of serious solemnity, I find myself talking, crying as my mother took the pain of her life, hunger, and poverty. I still want to live like a child of my mother's grace, with her security.

In the silence of the jungle I shall come to your cottage and you shall tell the stories of the beheaded kings, for not frightening me, for not haunting my peace. The stories of wars give a little calmness of graveyards; and we all have to reach there soon.

This moment is beautiful like a child carrying a lit candle and progressing towards the church, like the silence of the blue sky in the summer afternoons. In this quietness, there is the sum of the whole life. I would never miss this beautiful moment for an unknown future. Once this moment is lived, it will be prodigious.

When I sit under a mango tree during the early summer afternoons in solitude, something makes me aware of the existence of somebody other than me around. Those are the winds coming from all four directions with a nice song of a bulbul—the song of the youth, the song of life. And I still do not know from where it comes and to where it goes.

When I look into the heaven, sitting near a graveyard of my dear one, I suddenly find my sorrows to be my finest joys which remain till my thought process exists. And misery and happiness live together till the end. When my mind takes rest, then 'You' act upon. When both I and You take rest, the existence becomes the lone perspective.

The flute is played. The strings of the Sitar have been struck and the consciousness regained.

Let it wave with the sounds of the music and of the bees.

The fountain will flow. We will see ripples of happiness some day when the small child will gather little stones to make the walls of happiness tough enough so as not to be broken.

The way I lived my life in the saddest of moments or ecstasy were all my thoughts which started from the edge of my life, sometimes persuasive to give peace, sometimes glue the mask of happiness. At last I am just my thoughts as those moments pass away. No event can make us good or bad. It just brings us near to our own self.

I often talk to myself to become a king, and it has always made me realise later that it is all nonsense. So I left the idea. I thought to become a poet of no writing, and it was also not plausible. Sometimes sitting alone in an open field I started thinking my poetic powers and I found myself in excitement. So I thought it is always better to think rather than write badly. And I started writing a little later; it was either because of my inclination towards literature or of anger for the society. Everything I wrote were my pain and pleasure.

Long was the mountain range; thick were the trees of the jungle, fragranced was the air, whistling was the flow of fountains, and there was an assurance of a huge blue sky and all those with sleepless nights, days of loneliness.

No regret, there is a search of freedom of mind, if not anything.

Talks, gossips, truths, betrayal, all happen in war fields and temples. I call myself with another name, truly of that in the day of meeting possibly a moment of depart with nonsense humanity and the law of weaponing. Now my heart is laden with a fruit of only some seeds, my desires are blotted, and a treasure of silence is prevailing, if not anything else.

The seeds were sowed a season ago; not remembering, I walked through, the clouds showered, and the seeds grew for harvesting. Sunset was in the horizon and the night came with a lantern. Much I could not talk. Lot I could not hear. Friends are awaiting and some have speechless love, some tearless cries. All were ready to harvest; it was a sunny day. All were murmuring incoherently but with some truth. We shall transfer this truth to millions if not anything.

Everything for a crime or a cause is existentialism. It is there within us, and we should utilise it for the betterment of self, and then probably a little more peace can be achieved even in a war field. You and I talk a lot to the world for a human cause. It would make a better world if we ever tell something to ourselves.

The journey of life passes through many facets in a palanquin . . . . Night is there for a few minutes, where you and I live along. Few illusions we know, the truth unveiled . . . . Millions of happy moments are waiting ahead in the journey of life . . . . The journey of life is in the custody of death; here you and I see many facets of life . . .

Your heart needs no place other than in your mind which travels between the subconscious and unconscious. And it is you who can make your mind the absolute truth. If you are in the sky around the stars and planets, don't make your movements in vain. The clouds are conversing with each other, flowing with togetherness, and a glance of that can take you to a new horizon. The subtraction of your ego from the subconscious mind will save you of being sapped by the high tides of the ocean.

I cried to know myself and tried to make believe others the ways to get out of their miseries and make a better world. *Beyond poverty there is life enriched with heaven and earth, but the search is less.* My journey started and settled in the horizon where the heaven and the earth both find a place in the soul. We live in solitude and apprehension with lost hopes. We might have generated some impulsive suicidal ideas, but the world has never been in anguish because of us. It's as though we betray our own self. *Let us forget those lost hopes. We can make a better life and a better world, and that is what many a times I talked to myself.*

The sky is open; the earth is free to speak something.

Today the school is closed; it is holiday time and children are dancing, playing with joy and the sky is empty. The earth is free for them. Today the school is closed.

Today the sky and earth are free to speak; the river is anxious to merge with the ocean. Today children are fearless and playing with joy. Today the school is closed.

I started life's mysterious journey one day, and on the way through the journey there was nothing else but only a light. I passed through mountains, monarchs, and monasteries. I felt a hidden love everywhere, which surpassed the limitless mysterious path of life. All these things happen in life with grief and glee. Some flair and some flee.

People cry for their survival and of delusions. Nothing separates the moment of birth and death. I hear a million sounds and talk to one that comes from nowhere. I can make out those. I cry for every sound, and tears drop for the music that starts from within. And that is why I talk to self and cry.

Let me be alone and not feel the absence of others. Let me not feel the happiness because of others. I shall be happy when there will not be any casualty because of others. Let me be happy for my own sufferings.

You talk about the holiness of mind and soul. You pray in a church for not crucifying others, master the degree of preaching, and yet you cannot stop your anguish of selfishness. I heard some holistic speech given by a fisherman in the fishing boat, and it underwent the current of the tide and the smallest of the fish swam. At last I assured myself that people live for greed and hunger. The world has become impatient and merciless for which people live in greed and grief. Some day I shall find a way away from all this, and that would be something other than this world.

All have never gone. A peaceful sleep is still waiting, and that can only happen when the last need is satisfied. A part of Taj Mahal was broken. It was made with an intent 'the love' unlived, passed quietly. He made the Taj Mahal to refurnish the love which was even more intense than what was in the real life. *When the tower hold its head touching the blue sky, the king was dead.* He lived on deathbed, and the Taj a token of love. Now we made the Taj a token of heritage. No flower is thrown at, no worshipper enters her door. *The love is still there in the monument, and the king will meet again 'The Love'. So you stay alive, the Taj Mahal.*

I passed my happy days in talking to self, buying little ornaments for some loved ones and lost those the next morning. Grief took over the entire day, and the night passed with a disturbed sleep. I surrendered myself to the huge existence. I got up a little late in the morning. And the flowers had already blossomed before the sunrise. Now they are near me all around and will blossom all through my life.

A little recreation may give you joy at times, not a serene mood. A little money can give you many gifts but not solace. A little wealth can make you a king but never free you from worries. A person who knows a little reading and has a thoughtful mind is happy. A single moment of silence can make you enter into your soul. And I started reading and rehearsing all those which may cherish my last cry.

To the universe with the blossoming flowers of mid-winter, I am sending my cheerful thoughts to spread fragrance a little more from the deep forest to the noise. One day I shall depart from you and the colours of my clothes will change, my words will disappear. But the next winter when I shall blossom in your garden with someone's care, it will spread my dearness to you. I shall be next to you as a little bud waiting to open up.

I can feel my emotions. I can justify my prejudice. I can be a little surprised of my achievements. But I cannot just believe miracles without putting my intelligence into it, even though they seem true.

I know surely that one day I shall stop breathing and my heart will stop beating. People will take me to the graveyard. Some may grieve; some may soon cremate me following rituals. Even after long rituals, the day will take its part; people will again go to their jobs, and they may remember me for a day or two. The wind will blow, flowers will blossom, and there I shall stay forever. At the end of my life, all the achievements will be for a lost cause and my failures will show me the path ahead.

Stars would still twinkle in the sky, love would still pierce through the hearts of millions, and these are little things to ponder, but this is what we would miss in life. Everything would still not be lost yet. I would be enjoying meditation in my grave.

Till I was there with all of you, it was a circular journey. Now that I am departing, I say goodbye to all my obligations. I am making my journey straight into the universe where I shall closely observe you lighting the little lamp wherever darkness will come your way. Take care of all my love I showed to all of you.

I searched here and there for a loved one. There was nobody from the bay and beyond. Someone who was seen a little close was a passer-by who never stayed near my heart. And apparently, he passed away the next morning. I was crying in front of a mirror and found the other crying. And that is the moment I found somebody very close to me. And for all reasons, that 'somebody' loves me.

The beauty of life suddenly came to be seen to me; it happened when I came to a castle of budding plants, murmuring bees, and there I could not hear my sounds, only a few murmurs. Those were not of bees but of the cascade of life, and since then it is life everywhere for me.

I started my journey to a kingdom where people used to live with feud of feudalism.

When I approached the first village, the chief of the village told me: 'If you want to live in this village, we can provide you a big land.' I walked towards the central zone of the state. The king's order bearer offered me a job, provided I would stay there. I smiled at them and walked towards the palace, but the king put me in the jail for not being compliant to the state's rule. *I went a little ahead and found a child smiling at me. He said that if I played with him, he would tell the king to leave me—and there I stayed till the end of my life.*

I made an entrance to the unstructured eternity. I sat on the field of my assignment. I heard the song of the wind and then found myself at the feet of the master. And the master told me there is no salvation without knowing the self.

I spoke to the spirit of the mankind, and no reply came. I spoke to my emotions, and people were biding those without cost. Yet I must tell you, we all are passers-by, and we find ourselves lonely and aloof in a close-ended road. We start our day not where we ended yesterday; our friends get new ones tomorrow, leaving us alone. Our enemies make more of those. My friends and followers will be fewer and my love be forgotten. And then I shall take birth to speak to you more about love till you unlearn the anger. It may take a million years, and the darkness of delusions may make you unable to see my face, but I shall not hide from you. My voice may not be audible when my death will come, but the silence of my graveyard will tell you the truth of my love.

You and I

We all have gone through wakeful unconsciousness, through the sleeping nights of fading dreams; we have seen you in between the birth and death, the health and illness. The ambience of your silence left aside, we have put many swords in between your adorned wings. For more than your love for millions around us, we justify you better but in serious bloodshed. Many have pruned you. The meaning of our love in hidden motives is some pleasure and little persecution. Still you come with nakedness like a child; you laugh and weep, and you perish in sunlight, if not anything else.

I saw a war inside me and my thoughts building a house of wilderness. Often in the dreams of my loneliness, I struggled for peace. I told myself to hunt the merciless behaviour of people around me. I smelt the fragrance of earth in my twilight dreams and saw the beauty of thorny herbs, stony roads up to the holiness of the sky. When I woke up, I found my dreams were bigger than my belongings and my sorrows were tinier than the devastation the earth faces with every changing climate. I sat under a tree with an egoless mind and found my house bigger than all my life's miseries.

When I saw a little fish swimming in the ocean, I jumped into the ocean to catch the fish, and it took me deep down where I found millions of pearls. *And there I understood that you 'the artisan' can be seen deep in everything, even in death.* When I saw a silent bird flying in the huge blue silent sky, my mind rushed to catch hold of it, and then *it took me to the angels, where I found you smiling. I then understood you can even be there in a puzzled mind but deep in it.*

I remember you all, of not pain nor of owing you but of my unconscious remembrance. You cried with agony and that prevailed as of now. My dear part, I have a desert in my bosom with a flowering plant, and I offer it to you with all humble words. My day long struggle for living, love, and luxury are invisible when the evening deepens. My credits and credentials of a lifetime are just like waves of the wind. Every event in life either external or internal are the possessions of body and mind and beyond both the absolute remains. This realisation possibly would be the reunion of the body and soul. Hope life's fragrance will spread in my breath and the autumn will whisper in the ears of the winter to spread the petals of rose and willfully fall in the earth.

You are the unseen power that does everything good or bad. A misdeed done by me sometimes is when you whispered me to do. A million can smile with all thy words. People ambush their own in deserts and ocean. Give them a little passion to know what life is. It's my pleasure to be your art. I can make a few arts of yours alike, maybe washable.

I have seen you by not seeing. I have heard you by not hearing. O Lord! People say you are somewhere between the sky and the earth. Yet they try to crush the sky and burst the earth. Give them a little whisper to wake up and spread their hands to make a circular heart. O Lord! People call you . . . 'the Saviour'. Yet they destroy *thy love,* so beautifully spread over the Himalayas and the Antarctic. The artisan is murdered by your people. Teach them a little art of playing with a child and making some sand houses, paper boats, and that would make the world more peaceful.

Let us not dishonour you by not knowing the glory you created by showing the glimpses of your presence and the little things around. Let us not destroy our own, reject the beauty you have shown. You make your presence in a flower and we miss to feel you and your fragrance. And that is of life. You never betrayed us, never acted as a traitor. We consider the slightest of mishaps as your punishments. The wars that have destroyed the world are all in your name. Even after a war, you make the war field more peaceful. Mankind has discarded you in many ways, and yet you have given them the crown.

I sat on the shore of a roaring sea and looked up to the sky and far to the horizon. Again my sight came down to the earth, and I closed my eyes—it was a little light. It was a serene silence, and there was a little child playing with innocence. There was nothing else but a little murmur.

In silence the human race slowly progresses towards the time zone, moving relentlessly . . . . In silence the emotions blossom, the untold reveals. We touch the sky and make a shelter in the heaven . . . In silence we travel near each of our heartbeats and find ourselves in solace . . . The silent mountains and the sky unravel the mystery. And the silent smiles speak the truth, the truth of the human race.

In a summer afternoon sitting under a pine tree near the seashore, I felt the silence of the existence, the belongings of my emotions. And some voice came through the clouds whispering, 'All happenings are with you, but nothing belongs to you. You behave like a priest and may furnish your coat with a flower, but they are not like you. All through your life you say to give your belongings to the poor, but those were not yours, rather your perishable possessions. If you do not have greed for your possessions those may remain with you all through your life.

When I cried in painful agony during the race of life, at times it created hatred, at times hostility. As time passed, I faced life at different angles with turmoil and happiness. Tears soaked on the lips with the sweetness of music you provided in my voice. I see you always and hear you whisper every time I sing a song. These songs must have touched your feet like the waves of the ocean strike the shore. *I know you must have felt these words of the songs not only lyrical but full of innocence.* This is the way I have sailed from the west to the east. I am sure my Lord exists as my heart is still beating.

We do not have feud. There is neither the fierceness of hatred nor grimacing. But we all live in rivalry. Who is there for it? Nobody other than me. I can only try to make others wrong if I do not love myself, and to prove others right, there is nobody other than me. It's a must to love one's own self. And there would be nobody in person. Only the fragrance of life would be there in the air, and to enjoy all these, there would be nobody other than me.

I hope my tears will come down to the earth and touch your holy feet and find a way to the ocean. My agonies will perish with the spring touch of your fragranced air, with little flowers nodding here and there. The holy strings of a harp will sound at your garden. My happiness will find a way to the heaven, and I shall fly with the flock of birds to find a way to your door. There I shall see only your holy feet.

I started my journey towards happiness, leaving all conflicts and found the last bereaved one cherishing the pleasure of past defeats. I realised the existential state of life rather, trying for a false progress of achievement, and at last the angel seen and all other are needless. I hope one day the disenchanted, dejected, and belligerent people will come to see the flowers, taste the fruit of the plant which God planted many years ago. Sufferings, illusions, and the cry for life will be there, but we can face it.

You have given emotions to every life. It is with me too. You have punished all by making them to do something wrong. You whispered in everyone's ear regarding the sobriety of our act. Some stuck and a few struggled, while a very few reformed themselves. You whispered in my ear many times, but I could not listen because of the relentless mental activity. But you are still there with me all through my life. Please excuse me for all my idiotic innocence.

And there is a sky, an earth, and the ocean. I could not see my Lord who is always with me. O Lord, I have seen you when I was dreaming. When I am in silence, I sing a song, and I talk to myself. When I talk to you, I forget my consciousness.

We live in anguish of war, a merciless attitude of greed and grievances. We dance in footless movements, fall in the darkness of sin. We crush our existence and crumble the fate. Now is the time; today is the date. There is a flicker of rays from the unseen, and we may rise over the crusade. The splendour of life exists; just let it touch our soul. The miser will flee, and mercy will play the art of divine. And at last a little teardrop will wipe away the stains from our faces and the nectar will shower.

I shall not but some may cry when I shall be unseen in the mist of the winter night, and few may fall on the dusty road walking in haste to see my shroud. Few may throw some petals of red rose, few shall drop tears. The next morning all will go to their job, and I shall remember you all. My heart will beat to give you a wake-up call for a life ahead. Those will be like little shadowy clouds which will come through your windows, and I shall be there in the clouds giving a little love to flourish true emotions in your heart. I shall be there near you.

I know my visit to this planet is coming to an end. I want to come to the open field where I can feel your cool breeze, look at you through the clouds which ruffle the air a bit and to see your childlike smile. I can bear all those tragedies as I have broken my shell. You have taken all care through my journey till now. Now the rain has started falling down, and the clouds are already making their way. We will be there for many years from where we can look upon to the earth.

Love is my heritage. It was with my parents and forefathers; it will be with my loved ones. *Thou make us enriched with it.* Sometimes I forget to look at the hermitage. But the seeds of love which you sowed have already become plants and are branching enormously. *We are lucky to have love without cost.* It comes to everybody from somewhere. It came to me from the empty sky, mighty ocean, green jungles, blossoming plants, and soothing breeze. *We are lucky to have love without cost even when we face boisterous tides.* Some of those make us lost, some strengthened. For people to ever feel love in their heart, it must first blossom in their soul.

THE SECOND BIRTH

To me, the second birth means perception of life after I joined with eternity in my consciousness.

Every life contains hundreds of stories, millions of events. Each event is filled with different emotions and means something to the concerned.

I lived my life from the cell membrane to the nucleus. I sustained all injuries which the exterior gave me. I bore all my pain and pleasure. I could stand tall before all with all odds.

I have had my agonies and pleasure, smiles and seriousness. All those are too little or too many today and do not matter now. I have learnt how to put my foot on those stony roads.

I have always waltzed with them, and their gospels inspired me till now to live. People may put fire beneath my feet, but they can never imagine the agonies and all the emotions I have gone through.

And yet I can assure them of my serenity. Whosoever has a comment, good or bad, must never forget the path I have come across with the Almighty.

Feel all these and the next day I shall meet you near a temple or a graveyard. And you better not comment anything, as you know nothing about anybody who has walked with the Almighty. You try to know your emotions and then can join me, also the universe.

So many lyrical words have come to my lips in a frozen cold night. My heart is surrounded by the snowfalls. I searched for my breath but it had vanished; I did spread my arms to tie up my forgotten dreams. I searched for my dear emotions in the prison where all of us were chained then.

O my dear air,

For my love, open the prison and leave them who are so dear to me and you. Let them feel the baby sunlight, let them steal my dreams. I am still the king of the universe under the shadow of the wings of an eagle. I can take their sufferings. O my dear all, open the prison and let them sing and dance in the frozen cold night.

Love is the gospel of the Lord. I live to learn the art of love, and my life needs nothing except with love to merge with the Lord, so that neither there remains the Lord nor I.

I bow my head before you, the love of the Lord, which nourishes the soft seeds of the fruit. The fruit of the heaven, the beautiful life is enriched by you with your sweet wine.

And to the life you always adorn.

Come the entire universe and join the hands, uplift the love which flows by the flood. We shall be helpless without it. Let the love live and the sorrows perish. And then I can see a life is there to cherish.

We are all born from the earth (love); we all go into this earth (love). You can get the worth of salvation I assure, if you fold your hands before the love of the Lord.

We listen to many stories from our mother; we sing many poems of life with our grandmother. The mother feeds the child from her milk-laden breasts. She enjoys the marital relationship. She takes her dead children to the graveyard. Listen to the pain of our mother.

Listen to the murmuring sound of the insects in the jungle; listen to the cowherd's song and the music of the waterfall. The birds do their bit, and I see them making love with each other in my dream.

I see the humans, birds, and animals; they all drink the wine of death in the glass of their own life.

127

Listen to all the mothers' cry, to all the fathers' aggression and agonies. See their sons and daughters kill people and run away from seeing people killing others. And all of us blame our God. We drink the hot wine, the energy booster, and yet we sweat of fear; we plan for laughter but drop tears of our blood.

Listen, those hungry men with shrunken abdomens, swollen eyelids. You search for the hope as a dead. You all so-called honest people take advantage of small children's stammering words, behaving as you are their mentor, and then crudely sexually abuse a young girl who has had her menstrual cycle for the first time. You crudely murder a brave young boy. So everywhere every night there is the music of a war.

I have seen all these happenings in the journey of life and taken a second birth.

The night is the magician. It dissolves all the sonnets, fears, and comforts. It sings a song which is finely tuned, and it spreads over the entire existence. It is not audible to those who are asleep in the midnight. Those who play, sing, and dance with the darkness of night, the serenity of night, are the blessed. And those who forget about the night and sleep are only approaching the death. They are the blessed ones who alone feel the silence of night, who play hide-and-seek and run to the horizon with night. They are the brave and bright.

The earth is encircled by its beauties; the air and the nucleus of life are encircled by the Almighty. The Almighty is encapsulated by the entire process of life. Here the Almighty might be as small as it could be, but his description is as same as the universe. Everywhere in the smallest of the eggs/cells, the monitor is the unseen. If we can derive another nucleus inside that unseen, there would be the same Almighty.

Life can only be explored and enlarged if we discard our words and knowledge. Words can never take you to the periphery. I have come out of that egg, and the Almighty is there waiting for me.

We all have taken a bigger structure from that smaller one, from the little Almighty to the expanded Almighty.

A self-actualised individual touches every individual's life because he can understand his life. He remains with millions but alone and out of this world.

In every birth, we are transforming ourselves from better to best as the miniature Almighty always progresses in its form and flows till it merges with the universe. It can never remain imprisoned, so it always works and shows its magnanimous expansion.

I am now breaking the shell, and this would be my second birth.

Most of us reject our last freedom by ignorantly working against that finest energy which works within us. People who have recognised their destiny never fight with time, wasting their life energy. It is quite possible that we can dismiss the unreachable distance during this small life. So there is a chance of second birth always.

We all live one step at a time, and to earn life, we completely merge with what we do daily in routine. And the life remains a bit handicapped. We then become infected with different diseases. Life then comes to an end. But there remain a few fortunate ones who not only try to live bodily but also at the level of soul. And life takes its rebirth: it is 'the second life'. It happened to me when I heard the sweetness of my master's voice, although I never saw him. He left his mortal body many years ago when I found a place in his dynasty. But the oneness of my feelings with my master made me to learn about the eternity. And this is my second birth.

The root of all pain, sorrows, and worries of human life is that man always tries to be what he is not. The reality becomes unacceptable for him. We always think psychotic to achieve or become what we are not. People carry their happenings wherever they go.

Your acceptance of a particular thing makes it a different asset. You accept death; the quality of death will change, and during the course of death, you get a second birth, the birth of a new human.

Lao Tsu says, 'A person, wherever he is, should accept the happenings in his surroundings so that there will be no unhappiness.' He says, 'Your desire for future is a wistful destruction.'

The other day I asked my master, 'Is love a bond, and if so, are we all in a prison?' The master replied; 'No, love can make you free from all bondage and you can get a second birth. When you love every object, you do not have any bondage, and when you look back to the same heart from where it took birth, you will find the heart full with love and the unconscious ego clash will perish and you are free for a second birth.

When you are left only with love, time can only remind you regarding the same.

Your thought process and time are two variants of the universe. You are never alone. You are with your thought process and the concept of time. There is a transaction of thought and time with everybody.

A human being is miserable because his memory is very short. It cannot go with thought and time foot by foot. The short and unstable memory is the illusion of thoughts regarding life and death which you have made an account of. Time never negotiates with anything. It is pre-prepared, like life and death.

Each unit of life and death and their energy unites with the energy of the Almighty. So you are never absent from this universe.

God spreads his splendour with time everywhere. The wish of a tiny particle according to its little wish gets the same as the most developed human being's desires. No human being's desires are fulfilled ever, because in the unconscious he had different desires. At the end, there remains a space in mind. We should wish the love of others to flourish. And this will make our wish close to God's wish.

We are miserable because we wish to change our fate and happenings at an unconscious level.

You cannot enter into the wish of God till you do not know your own wish, and till then God's wish is a mystery.

You accept those who are not known to you, and they will help you to learn their secrets. There you shall take a second birth.

THE SECOND DEATH

For sure we will die, and, more importantly, we are not living today.

Deep in every act, there exists a life force (libido) or the act of sex. People eat to keep their own self alive, and people have sex to keep mankind alive. Immanuel Kant says, 'To keep celibacy is anti-life because you are killing the life cycle.' He says, 'The law which everyone can follow is genuine, and if not, it never has to.' If everyone follows celibacy, there will be no life. According to Kant, keeping celibacy is violence. But it has got its own limitations as Kant is only thinking life ends after death.

Mahavir says to keep celibacy is restoring energy to reach the other world where the consciousness is pure and away from the body. One can attain meditation and salvation without any struggle with celibacy. To enter the world of salvation is to come close to self, whereas sexuality is to go away from self.

All types of sexual and sensual urges are slavery, while celibacy is freedom.

We search for the contradictions to keep our identity intact. But Mahavir says, 'The search for salvation should be a search for self and death will be peaceful, and to search one's own self, one does not require the other.' Similarly life requires death. Death should not be a search, rather the ultimate inner growth.

All external growth creates aggression, and all internal growth creates peace.

To enter the path of death or a supreme life, you should follow: Now there is no hope, no future, no desire, only renunciation is liberation of life and entering into death which is a new life. No hope should remain now because all your hopes will lead you to a miserable death.

People do one thing, either they believe or disbelieve. And these are anti-life, which leads to a non-existential death. You will know the truth of life and death only through your experience and realisation.

Yoga is death and also a new life.

Where do we go after death?

1. A part remains here at our own home, because some part of our body comes from earth (Earth elements).
2. Some part goes to the sky, to the planets (sky elements).
3. Water elements go to water.
4. The fire elements go to fire.
5. The air elements also have their part in the body and turn into air.

Every object and its finer elements are there in human beings. The entire universe is just one object. So we can make connections with the universe and its smallest parts.

Like you die after living a certain period, in the same way, you live in some other form after your death and the miniature Almighty changes its form, flow, and place.

Do we come again to this world after death?

In being detached from the world, we shall take something to the other planet which the planet will attract every time to its periphery, and this is why we have to come to the world at some point of time. Till we do not quit our desire, the phenomenon of our coming to earth will be repeated.

The second death is the final going away from this planet and can only occur by loving everything of this planet but without any desire. You keep love for the world, the world will make you free from its attractions.

God says:

I shall welcome you to the divine death when you will have the desire to enter into the aura of God. When you have that desire, you will be above the life of a human being. You will be a worshipper then. And for a worshipper, death is with essence of life and eternity. And that is second death.

This concept is a 'new religiosity' and based on the love to leave, certainly to celebrate.

> 'I want to make a heaven
> on the earth,
> A man wherever lives, dies
> should earn its worth.'

My dear friends, wake up, for the time is short—life is passing. It's now or never.

Do not fight with the mind; do not surrender to the mind. Just think that you are the king of your own. You do not have to prove it, because this will indicate that you are not sure of your supremacy. Tell yourself: 'I have listened to my mind so much, but I could not get anything. Now I shall listen to my heart, and then I can die peacefully.'

The master says; Leave your possessions, prejudices, and quit your beliefs. You have to go to the truth naked with empty hands and alone in the narrow path. Your code of laws, religious treaties, your holy gospels make you not hear what I tell you, and you shall only hear the echo of your own thoughts.

During the entire life, you just make efforts to save your mind by becoming delirious. Unconsciously you are fearful of your mind, and this is why you do not confront the functions of mind and willfully accept them, and then you keep yourself away from the truth.

The master says; Sleep is a behaviour of avoidance. The more you sleep, the more you shall be a slave of your mind and you shall never find the truth. You talk relentlessly inside your mind, and is why you are unable to listen to me. Stop talking to your mind and you can hear me. You shall find an unending blue sky opening the door, where you can enter into and have a peaceful death.

HAPPINESS

Life's only principle is to be happy, and your happiness is based on your action. Your happiness should be in your way. Do not consider others' happiness and the way through which they get their happiness. Mostly people choose to remain unhappy unconsciously, and psychologically there are profound reasons for it. A social learning behaviour becomes most critical for giving happiness or unhappiness to a child. If a child is unhappy and his surroundings are empathetic to him, giving affection to him, he generates love for others. When people give attention to a child, it results in giving nourishment to the ego of the child, and, hence, the desire for happiness increases. Every child acts miserably to get attention and to become happier later. This is the real politics of life, and it starts very early from infancy. At the same time, when you are grown up, you seem to be happy about others even if they act dubiously. So now you have to learn how to maintain your happiness. If you are euphoric and enjoying your life, people will try to prove you wrong. But if you are melancholic, nobody will experience the same melancholy, which is happening to you from the very core of your heart. The entire society is based on misery, and your ecstasy will make the society feel perturbed. But do not worry. You go on your own way for happiness, and that is the real way of living life. If you are blissful and happy, you cannot go for nonsensical arguments.

If you are happy, there will never be an unrealistic urge of hoarding money, and this will ameliorate you throughout your life.

The entire society lives on misery, and this is why every child learns to become miserable at first. To stay in misery is your lifetime investment. So you choose to be in misery. Contrary to this, to be in happy state of mind is easier than to be in misery.

Every society makes miserable people out of joyful creators. Every child by birth is smiling and happy. But during death, he is just psychotic. This is the gift of our fellow societal members.

A child, to begin with, is happy, and everyone should try to regain their own childhood ego. When a child becomes unhappy or angry, he becomes totally involved in it and his entire being, his entire energy, becomes his action, but the child remains the same beautiful child. He looks even more beautiful. There remains no conflict after he becomes silent, and his ego function is supported.

The principle is, if you merge with any type of emotion, you become the same emotion. You are just a blissful one, and, hence, if you are not satisfying your ego functions, you are unhappy. So be one with your ego. To be intensely involved with the present is eternal. And there will be a continuous flow of happiness.

The life is yours, the play of life is yours, and you are the actor. So play with wisdom. Do not ask happiness from any guru, master, or well-wisher. *If you can create your misery, you can also create your own happiness.*

Another principle to be happy is to make the *ego to let go*. People make others learn to fight with ego, and that is why you suffer. Truths can never be obtained by fighting with ego, and, for ages, this has been an utter ignorance.

To remove your sufferings, go with your present and your ego. The existence is never an obstacle for you. The existence, the nature, is your mother; she feeds you with all your odds, and, hence, she cannot be your enemy. And moreover, you are just an atom here; you cannot fight with the entire existence. So be in love with it.

For happiness, you do not have to quit anything; rather, you have to understand it. And then you will be always with the eternity, the nature. There have been many studies (psychophysiological) regarding *contact comfort*, and these show that when a child is away from the mother or a mother substitute, the child becomes irritable and physically weak. So it is ever true for everybody that the Mother Nature cannot be against you. If you quit something from the nature, you are the one to suffer. So go with your body and mind, the existence, and the labile ego.

In the hands of a doctor, the medicine in which it is written poison becomes nectar and saves people.

You seek happiness from a master, a pope, or a *maulabi*, and they tell you to go against many things which are a part of the nature. If you do so, you are belittling your happiness.

The only method to become happy is to let go with your ego.

You just let go with the existence. It will lead to a path which would be appropriate for you, and, for sure, you will be at home. Your ego (mental state) will become just a silent observer. And then all your miseries, anxious moments, and unhappiness will be vanished.

One day I talked to myself that the existence had shown so many of its facets, and from every facet, I have learnt. I hope I'll definitely learn another facet of life or existence when death will prevail. *Because this is the optimum hidden treasure which life can give.*

1. Money cannot buy happiness. Your problem is that you worry too much about money. (G. E. Baldwin, 1856)
2. Call no man happy till he dies. (Herodotus, 1545)
3. Cast off all your desires; you will find the perfect happiness. (Buddha)
4. Happiness from a job can be expected if:
   - the employee is meant for the job or
   - the employee is not doing much of the job than assigned.
5. You have no more right to consume happiness without producing it than to consume wealth without producing it. (Bernard Shaw)

The best way to remain being away from unhappiness is to stop thinking about happiness. You will discover yourself next moment winning the game. Once you discover yourself, you would be the happiest person.

Most of us become unhappy when we remember our past happy days during the stressful time.

The only thing you do is, you always remain worried for a meaningless life. The moment you stop worrying about your life, you will understand the best meaning of life ever since you have lived.

Happiness is a state of mind when you are free from pain and agony.

People remain unhappy due to the fact that they try to get happiness. So do not try to be happy; just be with happiness.

People remain unhappy thinking about others. If they eliminate the thoughts of those insignificant others, they may bring happiness into their life. Think about your own self; somewhere you will find happiness.

Happiness does not have a history, but rather a competent present.

Comforts cannot measure happiness. Happiness is the ultimate comfort.

Sadness is mostly because of the fear of loss of a loved object. Abraham-Freud conceptualized; If there is a loss of loved object, you feel as if a part of your body is lost and become handicapped. So the feeling of the loss gives a depressed feeling.

(1) detachment from the worldly elements and controlling five senses, (2) meditation to calm down the restless thoughts and to sustain attention to progress through happiness, and (3) controlling (mind) thoughts and behaviour through spiritual practices.

Bhagavad Gita says, follow these :

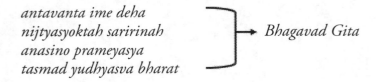

antavanta ime deha
nijtyasyoktah saririnah
anasino prameyasya
tasmad yudhyasva bharat

Bhagavad Gita

The above text implies that 'the body and all the materials of the world will perish one day'.

Happiness is beyond the perception of the word.

Happiness and pleasure make a right angle, in which happiness goes vertical and pleasure horizontal. Happiness comes from dissociation and pleasure an associational effect.

Happiness does not require a reason. It is just because of your thoughts. It grows vertically.

Think with your judgement and insight; you can realise how you can approach happiness.

Worries are the biggest enemies of humans. Keep worries at arm's length, spread the seeds of contentment in your mind, and generate passion for the heaven, and then your worries would be replaced by wisdom.

Faiths are rationalised behaviour which is used as psychological defence mechanism, and this should be explained to the client that he or she is using rationalisation as psychological defence and should come out of this and conquer fear, which is an overt illusion to stress.

We all are in transit and our persuasion of longevity is all in vain.

How can you be happy when you live in a house like a poison forest? There exist venomous snakes in great numbers, and you awake all night, sweating profoundly.

All shall perish a day or another, so do not snared by the illusion of the world. For happiness, just take a turn towards the saviour.

EPILOGUE

These are my spiritual ideas and are my single-parent children.

These are my thoughts without a mind, my nights without sleep, and my sleep without a dream.

These are my days without food and my evenings without tea.

All these are my wakeful unconsciousness, the road to the second birth.

These are my mistakes of holiness and the spartan life for a second birth. These are my sobriety after success and the sovereignty of slavery.

I sojourn here till the second birth.

And a day will come when the pages of this book shall open on its own and your eyes can make a mark of those. You can look into the words and phrases, and your quivering will stop upon reading as these pages tell you all the truths of life. You shall again close the book, and the pages will tear down with asphyxia in the closed space.

I shall tell you again not to read this book till I sleep peacefully in my grave, and the next day you must feel the missing of a daffodil.

GLOSSARY OF A FEW WORDS NOT FREQUENTLY USED IN ENGLISH

1. Tulsi—a holy plant
2. Aarti—hymns recited during worshipping God
3. Taj Mahal—a monument in Agra, India
4. Cold rice—used in some parts of India as a poor man's food
5. Osho—the great Indian philosopher master
6. Kabir—world's greatest saint poet who expressed maximum in a minimum of words known as *Doha* (couplets in English)
7. Rabindranath Tagore—the Indian Nobel Prize winner for his creation *Gitanjali*
8. Mahavir—a Jain saint
9. Lao Tsu—An Asian Master
10. Veena—A musical Instrument
11. Bhagavad Gita—The sermon of Lord Krishna (the holy book)
12. Abraham-Freud—two eminent psychological theorist
13. Contact comfort—a psychological concept of child development